HOGMANAY
Fun in Scotland

by **Julie T. Barringer**
Illustrated by **Judith Clymer**

Text copyright © 2012 Julie T. Barringer

All Rights Reserved

This book is dedicated to my dear departed friend, Moira Morrison

Thanks for our wonderful hours conversing about Scotland

Let's Celebrate

HOGMANAY!

Do you ever feel left out on New Years Eve when adults are celebrating?

The Scots involve all ages in

Hogmanay (pronounced "hog-muh-NAY"), Scotland's New Year's Eve and Day celebrations.

Hogmanay preparations, called "the Redding", start early on New Year's Eve. Everyone helps prepare. Many traditional Scottish dishes are baked to feed all who enter.

Here are some examples of traditional Scottish food.
Haggis: a meal made of a sheep or calf's inner organs boiled in a bag (from the animal usually) with oatmeal and spices
NEEPS: a neep is a root vegetable also known as a turnip, rutabaga, or swede, usually added to potatoes to accompany haggis
Tattie Soup: potato soup
Shortbread: a delicious biscuit made of flour, butter, and brown sugar (or white)
Tatties and Mince: a meal made of minced beef and potatoes(mashed or boiled), flavored with onion, garlic, and beef stock
Arbroath Smokie: a smoked haddock (type of fish)
Soor Ploome: a very sour plum flavored with boiled sweets
Stovies: another potato dish made with onions, carrots, beef, and sausage
Cock-a-leekie Soup: a dish made with of leeks, peppered chicken stock, rice or barley, and thin strips of prune
Clootie: a dessert dumpling pudding made with flour, dried fruit, sugar, spice, milk, and sometimes syrup

The entire home must be cleaned with all family members busy.

Fireplaces must be swept out and front steps

scrubbed clean (usually the children's job).

Even all debts should be paid from the past year.

The reason for such cleanliness is superstitions.

Superstitions
A cricket in the house brings good luck.
Opening an umbrella indoors causes bad luck.
A sprig of white heather is a good luck charm.
Breaking a mirror causes seven years of bad luck.
A sailor wearing an earring will never drown.
An itchy palm means money will come to you.
A cricket in the house brings good luck to all that live there.

The ancient Scots felt that it was bad luck to start a new year with a dirty house and debt.

As midnight approaches everyone becomes very quiet.

Village and city bells ring out twelve times to mark midnight.

Then, all the people nearby stand in circles holding hands

and sing the traditional song "Auld Lang Syne" written by Scottish poet Robert Burns.

Many cities in Scotland have huge festivals or parties filling the streets with well-wishers much like the Times Square celebration in New York City.

Now First Footing begins. This ancient superstitious custom begins as the 'first foot' steps into each home.  To have a dark-haired man be 'first foot' across your threshold (doorway) would ensure great fortune for the New Year.

However, if a blonde or red-haired woman approaches as first footer she would be shooed away since she signifies bad luck.

Members of families and neighbors come each bearing a symbolic gift.

These gifts might be shortbread or black bun (a fruitcake) so your family would never be hungry,

a piece of coal to signify a warm house,

or a coin for your pocket to ensure you great fortune.

As people come into your home they are offered all the food and drink they wish as a Welcome of Good Luck.

The tradition of New Year Resolutions also started in Scotland this way.

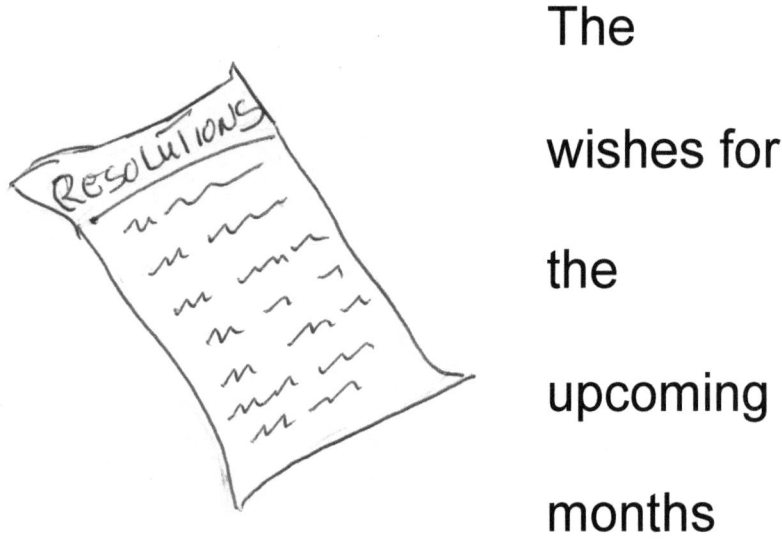

The wishes for the upcoming months would be shared by friends and family for each other and themselves.

Fireworks may explode in the skies at midnight.

After the First Footing has taken place and Scottish families have visited with others throughout the day, many continue their celebration into the night with bonfires.

Light from fires on this day symbolize lighting the New Year's path by

putting darkness in the past and looking forward to new adventures.

These Hogmanay festivities include everyone, young and old,

from the cleaning and baking to the bonfires of New Year's nighttime.

Wouldn't you love to participate in such a friendly, fun-filled New Year's celebration? Perhaps next December, YOU could start a celebration like this in your neighborhood!

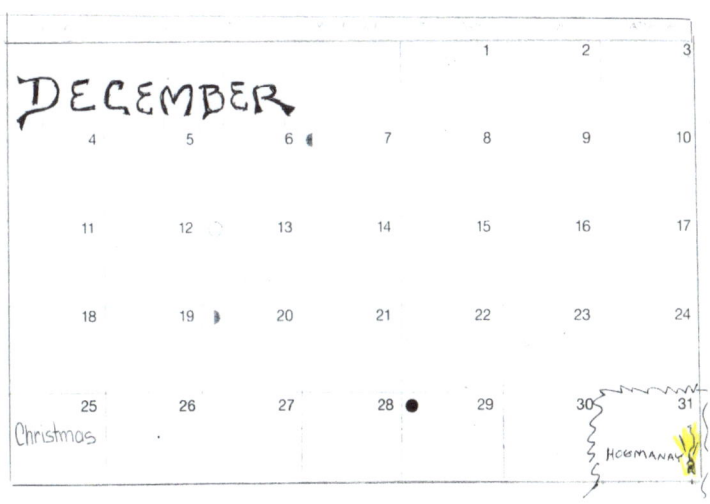

For Further Reading

Festivals in Scotland Frances Jarvce & Fhiona Galloway, published by Scottie Books 1999

The Wee Scot Book – Scottish Poems and Stories Aileen Campbell, published by the Pelican Publishing Co., 1994

Nessie – The Loch Ness Monster Richard Bassey, published by Orion Publishing Group, Ltd. 1996

The Story of Scotland Richard Brassey & Stewart Ross, published by Orion Publishing Group, Ltd. 1999

More Scotland Reading, Cooking, and Fun

***Christmas in SCOTLAND*,** published by World Book, Inc. 2002 A comprehensive description of Christmastime in Scotland, including details about Scottish Christmas celebrations, Hogmanay, crafts, carols and recipes.

Cooking the English Way by Barbara W. Hill, published by Lerner Publications Co. 1982 A cookbook for adolescents complete with cooking terms, menu example, and illustrations.

The International Cookbook for Kids by Matthew Locricchio, published by Marshall Cavendish 2004 This handbook begins with words on safety in the kitchen, a bit of history on some staple ingredients, detailed easy-to-follow directions, and an informative, illustrated section on equipment and utensils.

Classic Children's Games from Scotland by Kendric Ross, published by Scottish Children's Press, 2003 A book describing Scottish playground games.

Suggested Websites

Visit this website to enjoy games, stories, poems, jigsaw puzzles, coloring pages, and many other activities:
www.electricscotland.com

To learn about the history, people, and places of Scotland visit:
www.silversurfers.net/travel-daysoutscotland.html

Hogmanay Bibliography

Books:

Corrance, Douglas *Scotland: A Visual Journey* Mainstream Publishing 1999

Wormald, Jenny *Scotland: A History* Oxford University Press 2005

Internet sites:

www.aboutaberdeen.com

www.clansinclairsc.org

www.scotlandlogue.com

www.scotlands-enchanting-kingdom.com

www.edinburghfestivals.co.uk

www.google.com

Interviews:

Moira Morrison, native of Scotland

Sr. Brendan Harvey, SP, native of Scotland

(author's aunt)

several family stories handed down

www.ingramcontent.com/pod-product-compliance
Lightning Source LLC
Chambersburg PA
CBHW041809040426
42449CB00001B/33